CONTENTS

Some words are shown in bold, **like this**. You can find out what they mean by looking in the glossary.

HERE'S A TELEPHONE

All these bits and pieces make up a telephone. The small parts make the telephone work. They fit inside the large, smooth shell.

LOOK INSIDE

Telephone

Catherine Chambers

First published in Great Britain by Heinemann Library
Halley Court, Jordan Hill, Oxford OX2 8EJ
a division of Reed Educational and Professional Publishing Ltd
Heinemann is a registered trademark of Reed Educational and Professional
Publishing Limited.

OXFORD FLORENCE PRAGUE MADRID ATHENS
MELBOURNE AUCKLAND KUALA LUMPUR SINGAPORE TOKYO
IBADAN NAIROBI KAMPALA JOHANNESBURG GABORONE
PORTSMOUTH NH CHICAGO MEXICO CITY SAO PAULO

Designed by Celia Floyd
Illustrations by Barry Atkinson
Printed in Hong Kong

03 02 01 00 99
10 9 8 7 6 5 4 3 2 1

ISBN 0 431 08688 5
This book is also available in hardback (ISBN 0 431 08683 4)

British Library Cataloguing in Publication Data

Chambers, Catherine
   Telephone. – (Look inside)
   1. Telephone – Juvenile literature 2. Telephone – Design and
   construction – Juvenile literature
   I. Title
   621.3'86

Acknowledgements
The Publisher would like to thank the following for permission to reproduce photographs:
Chris Honeywell, pp.4–21

Cover photograph: Chris Honeywell

Our thanks to Betty Root for her comments in the preparation of this book and to Geemark
Telecom Ltd for their assistance.

Every effort has been made to contact copyright holders of any material reproduced in this
book. Any omissions will be rectified in subsequent printings if notice is given to the Publisher.

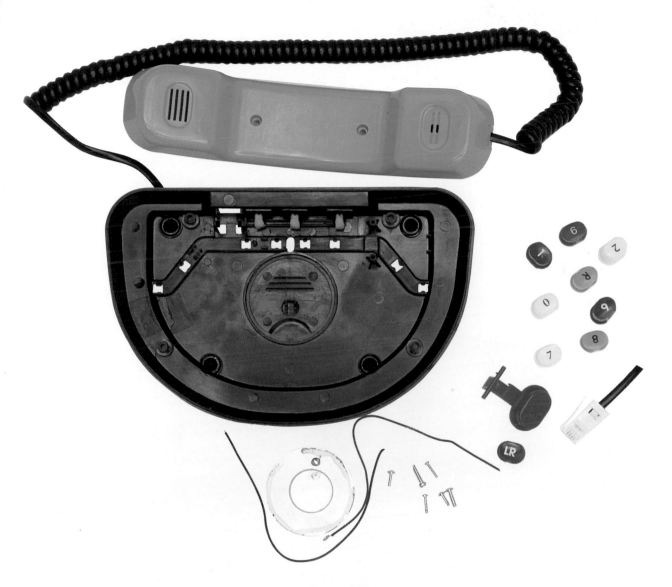

The pieces are made from different materials. You can see hard metal parts and **flexible** metal wires. There is tough, shiny plastic. There is thin, **fragile** plastic.

THE DIALLING UNIT

The dialling **unit** is made in two pieces. The bottom piece is flat. It covers the workings. There are spaces for each working part. Buttons and wires are working parts.

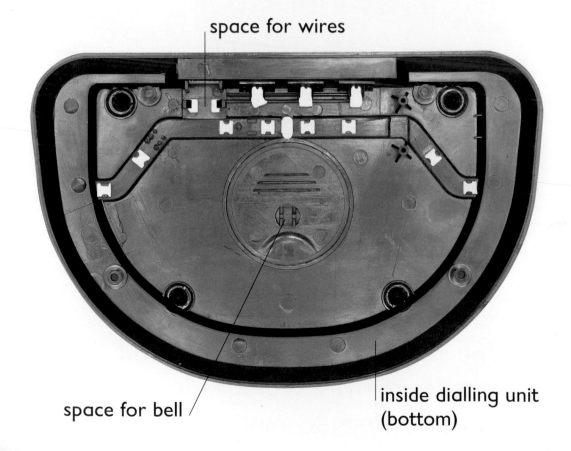

space for wires

space for bell

inside dialling unit (bottom)

The top half of the unit is curved. The receiver fits here. There are holes for the buttons. They are just a bit larger than the buttons. Both parts of the unit are made from tough, shiny coloured plastic.

curved space for receiver

outside dialling unit

spaces for dialling buttons

DIALLING A NUMBER

receiver button

dialling buttons

The buttons are made from tough plastic. They are close together. This makes the phone number easy to dial. Each button is set on a soft spring so it springs back quickly. But it is easy to push.

8

wires from buttons into telephone

Numbers are clearly marked on the buttons.
When you press them, an **electric signal**
travels through wires. The signal opens a
clear line to the other telephone. The signal
makes the other telephone ring.

RING-RING!

The ringing sound is made inside the telephone. An **electric signal vibrates** against a thin plastic disc. This is called a diaphragm. The diaphragm vibrates, too. It moves the air around it, making waves of ringing sound.

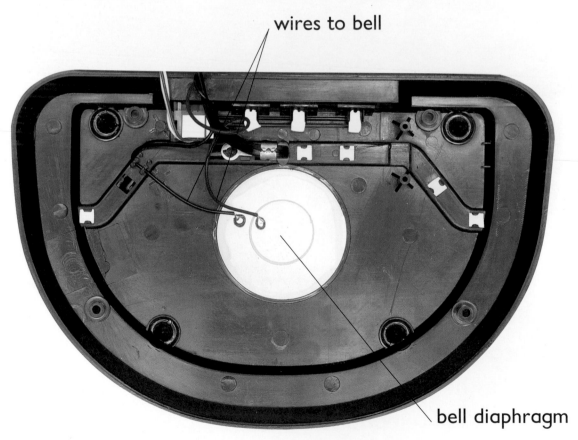

wires to bell

bell diaphragm

The receiver rests against a button. This button connects the electric signal to the diaphragm. When you pick up the receiver, the button springs back. The electric connection is broken so the phone stops ringing.

button is
pressed

connection
is made

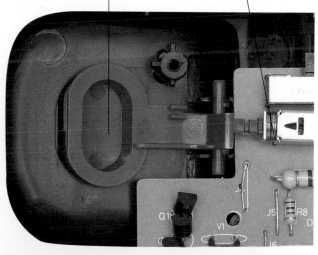

connection broken between
receiver button and bell

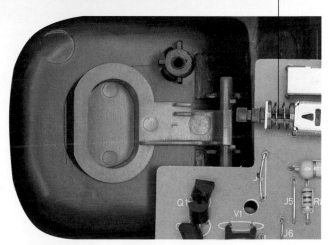

THE RECEIVER

The receiver is made in two parts. They are curved to fit around the side of your face. The mouthpiece and earpiece curl inwards. So they are close to your mouth and your ear.

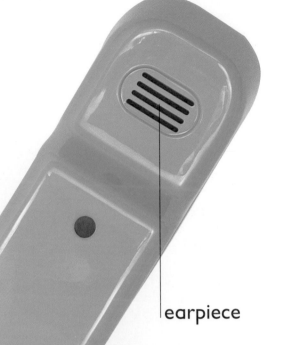

earpiece

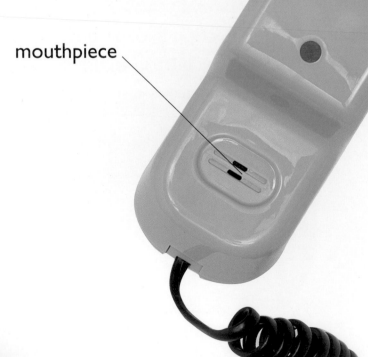

mouthpiece

Both pieces are made of tough plastic. The flatter part is like a cover. It clips onto the part with the workings, the mouthpiece and earpiece. These have slits and holes in them. This is so you can speak and listen.

inside receiver

cover of receiver

SPEAKING

Your voice is really waves of sound through the air. A microphone inside the mouthpiece turns your voice into **electric signals**. The microphone has a paper-thin disc. The voice makes this disc **vibrate**.

microphone

The disc presses against tiny grains of
carbon packed into a **cylinder**. An electric
current flows through the grains. The
pressure turns these into electric signals.
The signals then travel along the wires.

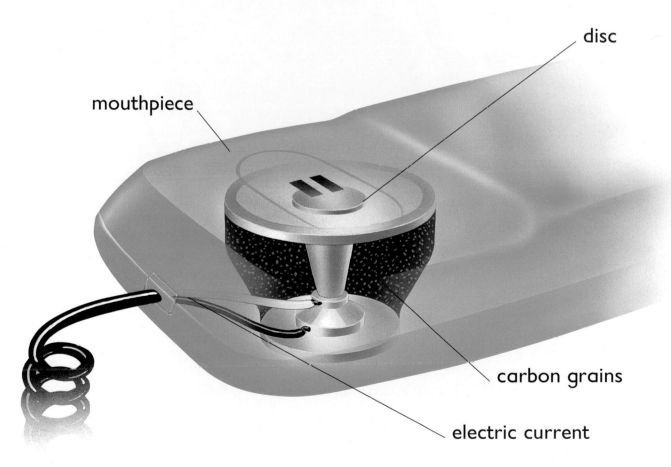

disc

mouthpiece

carbon grains

electric current

WIRES

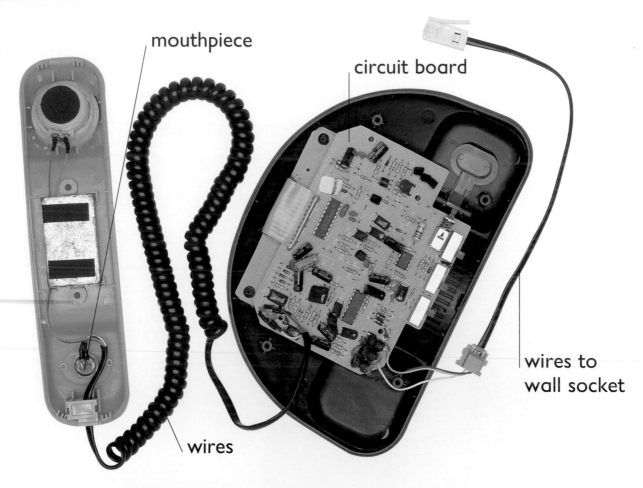

mouthpiece

circuit board

wires to wall socket

wires

Copper metal wires run from the receiver into the dialling unit. They pass along a **circuit board** and out to a wall **socket**. The wires are covered with coloured plastic. They go from your house into the ground.

Underground wires are often made of two solid glass tubes, called optical fibres. One tube is inside the other. The tubes carry the sound of your voice as light signals instead of **electric signals**. These bounce along the glass until they reach the earpiece.

inner glass tube

a single optical fibre

outer glass tube

light signals bouncing along

a bundle of single optical fibres

THE EARPIECE

Wires run through the receiver. They carry **electric signals** to the earpiece. The workings of the earpiece are inside a **cylinder**. Here, the electric signals move a tight wire **coil**. This is an electromagnet.

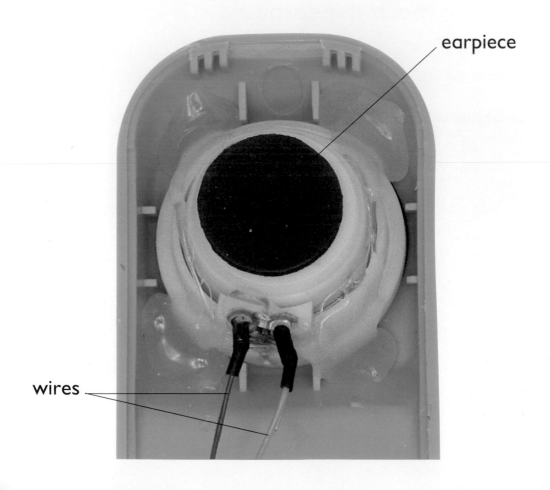

earpiece

wires

The electromagnet **vibrates** against a paper-thin disc. The disc vibrates and makes sound waves in the air. Now you can hear the voice!

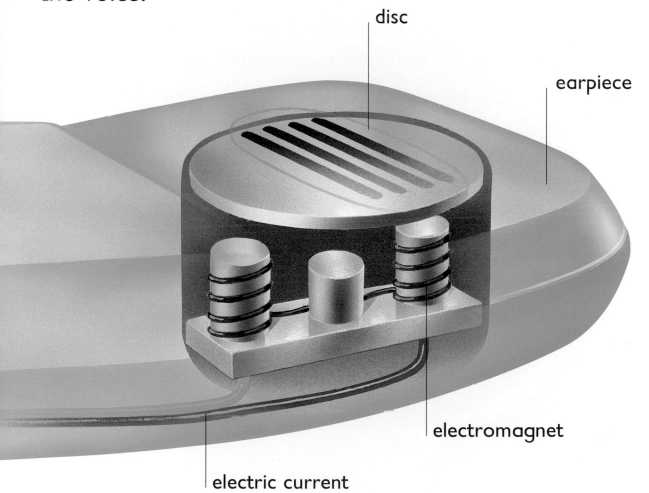

disc

earpiece

electromagnet

electric current

USING A TELEPHONE

Here is the telephone. It can fit on a desk.
Or it can be fixed to a wall. The receiver has
a curly, stretchy wire. So you can even carry
it a little way. Some telephones have no
wires at all. You can take them anywhere.

The telephone is ringing. You can pick up the receiver and hold it easily. It weighs very little. The telephone is bright and colourful. Its shape is smooth, curved and trendy. Enjoy using it to talk with a friend!

GLOSSARY

carbon   a gritty kind of stone

circuit board   a board that holds tiny switches and wires. These control the flow of signals from one part of a machine to another

coil   something that winds round and round, such as a spring

cylinder   something that is shaped like a tube

electric signal   a message produced by electricity

flexible   bends easily

fragile   breaks easily

pressure   the force of something pressing down

socket   a hole made for a plug

unit   a single working machine

vibrates   move backwards and forwards very quickly

Further reading

101 Questions and Answers: How Things Work. Ian Graham. Hamlyn, 1993

How Things Work. Steve Parker. Kingfisher Books, 1990

Science and Technology – A Visual Factfinder. Brian Williams. Kingfisher Books, 1993

Science and Technology – Black Holes to Holograms. Oxford University Press, 1993

INDEX